SHINING Star

THE ANNA MAY WONG STORY

BY PAULA YOO

ILLUSTRATED BY LIN WANG

Lee & Low Books Inc.
New York

Anna May Wong struggled to free herself. Tight ropes bound her to the railroad tracks. A plume of smoke puffed into the sky as a train rumbled toward her. . . .

"Stop daydreaming!"

Startled, Anna May opened her eyes. The train vanished. Steam, not smoke, hissed from a nearby boiler filled with dirty clothes.

"Get back to work!" snapped her father. "We have a full day's worth of laundry to clean and press."

Anna May sighed. No longer a damsel in distress in an exciting movie, she was just a nine-year-old girl toiling away at her father's laundry in Los Angeles's gritty Chinatown. Her sisters, Mary and Lulu, scoured clothes with washing powder against scrub boards. Younger brothers James and Frank squeezed wet trousers through squeaky cylindrical dryers. Her mother, with baby Roger strapped to her back, hung up clean dresses to dry on a rod along the ceiling.

Picking up a heavy iron from the coal-burning stove, Anna May felt the familiar ache in her arm. She saw the small burn scars that covered her hands. She longed to escape this dreary, backbreaking work.

When Anna May finished ironing the shirts, she put them in a basket to lug up the hill to customers' homes. After she completed her deliveries, Anna May counted five pennies in tips. That was enough to buy a movie ticket for the afternoon matinee!

There was nothing Anna May enjoyed more than sneaking away to the cinema. Watching a movie, she could escape from her everyday life, travel to interesting places, and experience new things.

Stashing her laundry basket outside, Anna May bought her ticket and slipped into the theater. Everyone gasped when the heroine of the movie was trapped in a sawmill. Anna May covered her eyes and peeked between her fingers. The heroine, with her hands and feet tied, lay on a moving conveyor belt headed toward the huge, spinning blades. . . .

Suddenly lights flooded the room. The movie had ended with a cliff-hanger. Anna May would have to wait until the following week to see if the heroine would be rescued.

Anna May wished life was like the movies. She dreamed of a hero coming along to rescue her from working in the laundry, and from the bullies at school.

Most of the boys and girls at Anna May's school were white. They taunted Anna May, yanking her pigtails and shouting "Chinaman" and other hurtful names. Her father told Anna May to stay quiet and not fight back. "Hold no malice in your heart toward anyone," he said. "We must be proud always of our people and race."

Anna May tried hard to follow her father's advice, but still she hated going to school. One morning as Anna May reluctantly dragged herself to school, she noticed a police barricade on Flower Street. Giant cameras and lights filled the sidewalk. A man aimed a camera at a woman dressed in rags. They were filming a movie!

During the next few weeks, the movie set became Anna May's new classroom. She regularly skipped school to watch the action on the set and ask questions about filmmaking. The amused actors and crew soon gave Anna May a nickname—the Curious Chinese Child.

Anna May loved this exciting world and wanted to be part of it. She decided she would become an actress. Instead of watching movies, she would star in them. She would be rich and famous so she could support her family. No one would ever have to work in the laundry again.

Every day, Anna May would rush home to reenact the scenes from the film in her bedroom. She practiced different emotions in front of her mirror. For fear, she gasped and collapsed to the floor. For anger, she snarled and curled her fingers into claws.

One evening Anna May's parents caught her weeping at the mirror, dabbing her eyes with a handkerchief. She confessed she was imitating the actors she watched at a movie set instead of attending school.

Furious, her father shouted, "You have to go to school! Not play hooky!" Actresses were looked down upon in traditional Chinese society, he said. "A good girl will not be an actress."

Anna May's father punished her, forbidding her from cutting school again. But no punishment could discourage Anna May from her dreams of stardom. Throughout her school years, she secretly visited movie sets whenever she had the chance.

When Anna May was a teenager, her father got her a job as a secretary. He hoped lining up a steady career for her after high school would end her Hollywood fantasies. Instead, Anna May was fired after only one week because of her poor shorthand skills.

Anna May grew to a height of five feet seven inches and she dressed in the latest 1920s "flapper" fashions. She cut her hair into a stylish bob with blunt bangs. She was beautiful and had many admirers. One was a movie director who needed three hundred Chinese men and women to work as extras in his film *The Red Lantern*. Anna May begged her father to let her audition for a part. She could earn seven dollars and fifty cents each day. Her father grudgingly gave his permission because their family needed the money.

Anna May was chosen as an extra for the movie. On her first day of shooting, hoping to look like a star, she dusted her face with rice powder. She curled her hair and rubbed several wet sheets of red-dyed Chinese tissue paper over her lips and cheeks. To her embarrassment, the director laughed and made her wash her face. Anna May was disappointed to discover her job was very simple. All she had to do was carry a lantern down the street.

Over the next few years, Anna May worked as an extra in many movies, hoping one day to be discovered and offered a bigger role. She never complained about the long hours on sets, and she followed all the directors' orders. Soon movie critics were praising her large, expressive eyes and ability to convey emotion with graceful hand movements.

Although Anna May's father still disapproved of her career as an actress, he admired her diligence. If he couldn't change her stubborn mind about Hollywood, he explained to his daughter, then he would do his best to help her succeed. Anna May's father insisted on driving her to all her auditions. He also suggested that she live at home. Instead of paying rent for an apartment, she could save her hard-earned money.

Anna May won her first big role in *Bits of Life*, a 1921 movie starring Lon Chaney as a Chinese man named Chin Chow. She played his wife, Toy Sing. To her shock, Anna May learned they were not allowed to kiss on-screen. Movie studios forbade actors and actresses of color to kiss their white costars because they feared audiences would disapprove.

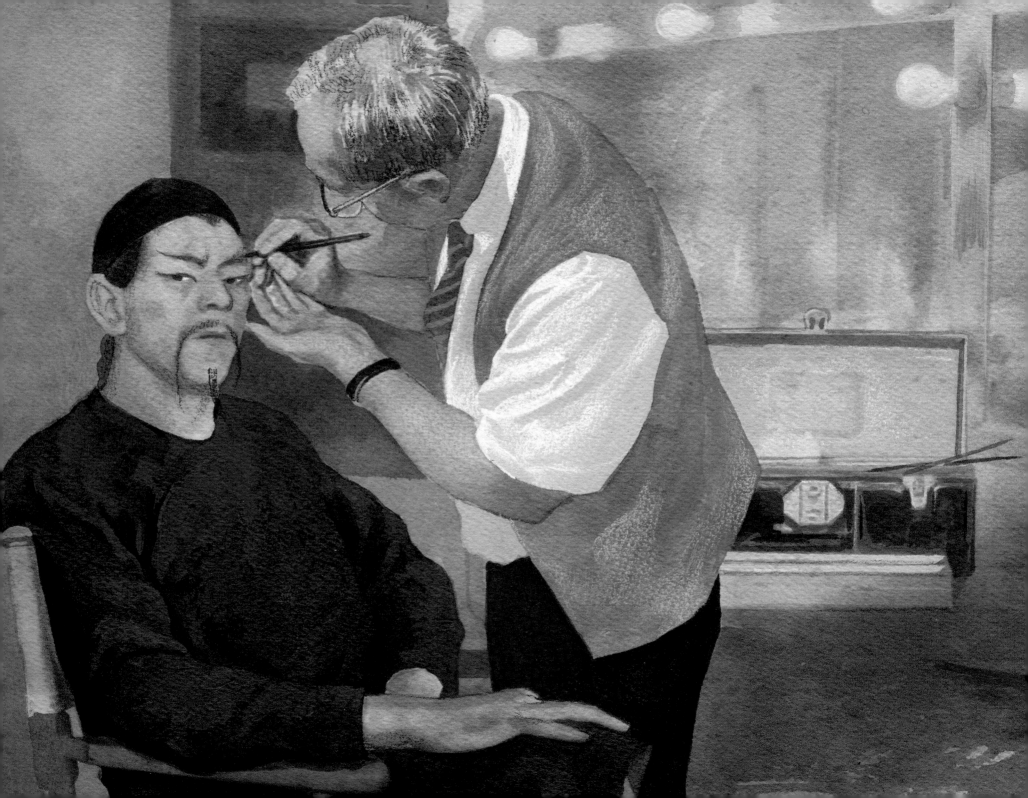

Even worse, Anna May saw a makeup artist dusting yellow powder on Chaney's face to give him what they claimed was Chinese skin coloring. He also used tape and spirit gum to pull Chaney's eyes into an exaggerated slant. This makeup was called "yellowface."

The yellowface makeup disturbed Anna May. Her father had always told her to be proud of her race, but the ugly makeup made her feel ashamed. She wondered if movie viewers would assume all Chinese people looked that horrible.

Still, Anna May was earning one hundred fifty dollars a week, money her family needed. She put her concerns aside and played the role.

In her next several films, Anna May won small supporting parts. Although she was proud to help her family with her earnings from these movies, she wasn't proud of the roles. Many of her characters portrayed Chinese women in a negative light and promoted stereotypes—from the scared and submissive "China doll" to the evil and domineering "dragon lady."

Anna May hated these demeaning images, but she could not afford to turn down the parts. Still, she always gave her best performance, hoping one day to play a dignified leading role. Frustrated with the roles in Hollywood, Anna May moved to Europe for a few years and won supporting parts in British and German films. In 1929, her role as a graceful dancer in *Piccadilly* made her an overnight sensation in Europe. People mobbed her everywhere she went, and European girls cut their bangs short like hers. She had finally achieved her dream of international movie stardom.

A confident Anna May returned to the United States in 1935 to audition for what was considered the most important movie of its time for Asian American actors. The film version of Pearl S. Buck's Pulitzer Prize-winning novel, *The Good Earth*, would depict China in a realistic manner.

Anna May wanted the lead role of O-lan, the loyal and kindhearted wife to Chinese farmer Wang Lung. But the role of Wang Lung had already been given to Austrian-born actor Paul Muni. In the script, O-lan had to kiss her husband. Because of the movie studio rule against interracial kissing, only a white actress could be cast as his wife. German-born actress Luise Rainer won the role.

Heartbroken, Anna May stood at a crossroad in her career. Her ethnicity was keeping her from achieving her dream of becoming a Hollywood star. She loved acting but was uncomfortable taking roles that presented racist images. She wondered why Hollywood and Americans accepted these unfair views. Was she doing more harm than good with these movie parts? "I'm torn between my race and my American homeland," she said.

Not feeling welcome in her own country anymore, Anna May decided to go to China. She would visit her parents, who had recently retired and moved back there. Although Anna May had never been to China, she was eager to learn more about her heritage. "I'm traveling to a strange country," she told reporters as she boarded the SS *President Hoover*. "And yet, in a way, I am going home."

Anna May arrived in Shanghai on February 9, 1936. Along with the thousands of cheering Chinese fans waiting for her at the pier were just as many Chinese people who resented her for playing movie roles they believed were disrespectful to Asians. A gracious Anna May defended her career, saying that if she was to be an actress, she often had no choice when it came to the parts she could play.

During her stay, Anna May absorbed as much Chinese culture as she could. She studied Chinese philosophy, attended a Chinese drama school, and took Chinese language classes. She went to fancy fifteen-course meals with ambassadors to help create goodwill between China and the United States. At a silk factory, Anna May was fitted for a traditional silk dress called a *cheongsam* to show her pride in her Chinese heritage. She also rode rickshaws, visited temples, saw the Great Wall of China, and signed autographs for eager Chinese fans.

In her family's ancestral village of Chang On, Anna May and her father talked for hours on the steps of his house. For the first time he opened up to her about his childhood in Sacramento, California, where he had worked in dangerous gold mines. She learned how much her father had sacrificed so their family could have a better life in America. Then he reminded her, "We must be proud always of our people and race."

Anna May understood her father better and felt proud of his accomplishments. As she gazed into her father's eyes, she realized he was proud of her too. Anna May decided that she would honor her father and her Chinese heritage by fighting for more authentic images of Asians on-screen. "I will never play again in a film which shows the Chinese in an unsympathetic light," she vowed.

Anna May kept her word. After returning to Hollywood, her first of many positive roles was in *Daughter of Shanghai*, released in 1937. She played a loyal, loving Chinese American daughter who solves the mystery of her father's murder. "I like my part in this picture better than any I've had before," she said proudly. "This picture gives the Chinese a break—we have sympathetic parts for a change. To me that means a great deal."

Anna May Wong looked forward to her future in Hollywood, playing parts she could be proud of. And for the first time in her life, she truly felt like a shining star.

AUTHOR'S NOTE

For the rest of her acting career, Anna May Wong accepted only positive roles, including the characters of Lin Ying in *Bombs Over Burma* (1943) and Kwan Mei in *The Lady from Chungking* (1942). Anna May donated money she earned from these movies to the China War Relief to aid Chinese refugees during the Japanese invasions of the late 1930s. She also auctioned off her extensive collection of ball gowns and sent the money and medical supplies to China during World War II.

In the 1950s, Anna May made the transition from movies to television, starring in guest roles on popular shows such as *The Life and Legend of Wyatt Earp* and the *Mike Hammer* detective series. She also starred in a short-lived TV show called *The Gallery of Madame Liu-Tsong*, about an art gallery owner/detective who hunted for art treasures.

Portrait in Black, the last of more than fifty films in which Anna May appeared, was released in 1960. Anna May never married or had children. In her later years, she lived with her brother Richard and owned several cats and dogs. She also carefully tended a large garden of exotic plants.

On February 3, 1961, Anna May Wong died in her sleep of a heart attack at the age of fifty-six. For many years after her death, her career was viewed in a negative light. Film scholars and the general public criticized what they perceived to be her stereotypical portrayals of Asian characters.

In recent years, however, many scholars and fans have realized how much Anna May struggled in her fight against discrimination in the movie industry. Critics now praise Anna May's ability to portray her limited roles with humanity and sympathy. Today, aspiring Asian American actors and actresses acknowledge her important contributions to improving Asian images on-screen. Anna May Wong said she felt "suspended between worlds" because of her Chinese ancestry and American upbringing. Her legacy bridged a gap between both worlds and helped open doors for today's generation of actors.

Photo courtesy of Anthony B. Chan, author of *Perpetually Cool: The Many Lives of Anna May Wong (1905–1961)*. Lanham, MD: Rowman & Littlefield, Scarecrow Press, 2003.

For Neil Levin—may your star shine brightly forever—P.Y.

For Megan, Nicholas, and Willson—L.W.

Acknowledgments
Special thanks to my editors, Jason Low and Jennifer Fox, for their wise editorial advice and guidance—P.Y.

Author's Sources
Chan, Anthony B. *Perpetually Cool: The Many Lives of Anna May Wong (1905–1961)*. Lanham, MD: Rowman & Littlefield, Scarecrow Press, 2003.
Chang, Iris. *The Chinese in America: A Narrative History*. New York: Penguin Books, 2004.
Hodges, Graham Russell Gao. *Anna May Wong: From Laundryman's Daughter to Hollywood Legend*. New York: Palgrave Macmillan, 2004.
Leibfried, Philip, and Chei Mi Lane. *Anna May Wong: A Complete Guide to Her Film, Stage, Radio and Television Work*. Jefferson, NC: McFarland & Company, Inc., 2004.
Leong, Karen J. *The China Mystique: Pearl S. Buck, Anna May Wong, Mayling Soong, and the Transformation of American Orientalism*. Berkeley: University of California Press, 2005.

Movies Viewed
Piccadilly (1929)
A Study in Scarlet (1933)
Lady from Chungking (1942)
Dangerous to Know: The Career and Legacy of Anna May Wong – Excerpts from a panel held at the Castro Theatre (March 7, 2004), featuring moderator B. Ruby Rich (cultural critic and author) with panelists Jacqueline Kim (actress), Karen Leong (author), Nancy Kwan (actress), and Graham Russell Gao Hodges (author)

LEE & LOW BOOKS Inc., 95 Madison Avenue, New York, NY 10016
leeandlow.com

Manufactured in China

Book design by Susan and David Neuhaus/NeuStudio. Book production by The Kids at Our House.

The text is set in 14-point Weiss. The illustrations are rendered in watercolor and acrylic.

10 9 8 7 6 5 4 3 2 1   First Edition

Library of Congress Cataloging-in-Publication Data
Yoo, Paula.
Shining star : the Anna May Wong story / by Paula Yoo ; illustrated by Lin Wang.
p. cm.
Summary: "A biography of Chinese American film star Anna May Wong who, in spite of limited opportunities,
achieved her dream of becoming an actress and worked to represent her race on screen in a truthful, positive manner"—Provided by publisher.
ISBN 978-1-60060-259-7 (hardcover : alk. paper)
1. Wong, Anna May, 1905-1961—Juvenile literature. 2. Motion picture actors and actresses—United States—Biography—Juvenile literature.
I. Wang, Lin, ill. II. Title.
PN2287.W56Y66 2009
791.4302'8092—dc22
[B]
2008042673